BLOODY BAYONETS

A COMPLETE GUIDE TO

BAYONET FIGHTING

BLOODY BAYONETS

A COMPLETE GUIDE TO
BAYONET FIGHTING

by

SQUADRON LEADER R. A. LIDSTONE
R.A.F.V.R.

Author of
" The Art of Fencing "
" Kendo : The Art of Japanese Swordsmanship,"
etc.

SKETCHES by

L./CPL. M. C. CLIFFORD
BEDFS. & HERTS. H.G.

The Naval & Military Press Ltd
© 2008

Published by the
The Naval & Military Press
in association with the Royal Armouries

Unit 10 Ridgewood Industrial Park,
Uckfield, East Sussex, TN22 5QE
Tel: +44 (0) 1825 749494
Fax: +44 (0) 1825 765701

MILITARY HISTORY AT YOUR FINGERTIPS
www.naval-military-press.com

ONLINE GENEALOGY RESEARCH
www.military-genealogy.com

ONLINE MILITARY CARTOGRAPHY
www.militarymaproom.com

The Library & Archives Department at the Royal Armouries Museum, Leeds, specialises in the history and development of armour and weapons from earliest times to the present day. Material relating to the development of artillery and modern fortifications is held at the Royal Armouries Museum, Fort Nelson.

For further information contact:
Royal Armouries Museum, Library, Armouries Drive,
Leeds, West Yorkshire LS10 1LT
Royal Armouries, Library, Fort Nelson, Down End Road, Fareham PO17 6AN

Or visit the Museum's website at
www.armouries.org.uk

In reprinting in facsimile from the original, any imperfections are inevitably reproduced and the quality may fall short of modern type and cartographic standards.

Printed and bound by CPI Antony Rowe, Eastbourne

CONTENTS

LIST OF ILLUSTRATIONS

INTRODUCTION

BAYONET FIGHTING is a bloody business; nevertheless, many of us may yet be called upon to tackle the enemy with this weapon as others have already done, so let us be prepared.

Some writers have asserted that Bayonet Fighting is an out-of-date kind of warfare and that the Tommy gun has relegated the bayonet to the museum. It is true that many new methods of destruction have been devised and developed since the last war, but it is equally true that during the present struggle and in all theatres of war the bayonet has proved itself to be a remarkably useful weapon when handled with determination and skill.

Hand-to-hand fighting still exists; a large number of our land forces are armed with rifles and bayonets, and when the occasions arise they do not hesitate to use them. If bayonets are as effete as those writers would have us believe, why are the Russian and German riflemen still equipped with them? And can it be denied that many a situation has been saved by the bayonet when ammunition has run out?

However, leaving it to the powers that be and their armchair critics to decide the manner in which our men shall be armed, one fact remains indisputable: many of them, whether they be in the Army, the Royal Air Force or the Home Guard, *are* armed with rifles and bayonets, and it is therefore essential that they know how to handle them efficiently and that they are well practised in the use of them.

CHAPTER I

To be successful in any hand-to-hand encounter it is necessary to possess two qualities : Determination and Skill, or the Will to win and the Ability to win.

The will to win is entirely dependent on the appreciation of the value of the cause for which you are fighting ; the stronger this appreciation, the greater the determination to achieve success.

The chief characteristics of ability to win are confidence, cool-headedness and experience, all of which are equally important. It is hardly necessary to observe that without self-confidence—or a superiority complex, if you prefer this expression—there is no chance of winning, but that with it there is every chance, especially if you convey to your opponent the impression that you possess it, and possess plenty of it. But it is important to point out that self-confidence must be tempered by cool-headedness, for over-confidence may spell disaster.

Experience may be gained on the battlefield or in the gymnasium. Initial battlefield experiences are certain to be extremely dangerous, but the danger is reduced to a minimum if full advantage has previously been taken of the experience of others ; that is to say, by training and, after training, by practice.

The first step in training is taken when the man is given a rifle and is taught how to slope arms. From then on every time he handles his rifle, every time he is made to do rifle drill, he is becoming more familiar with his weapon. He then advances to Bayonet Drill, where he learns how to attack in mass formation, and the offensive spirit, so essential to this form of fighting, is instilled into him.

Having gained an elementary knowledge of the use of the bayonet in attack, it is necessary to put this knowledge into practice, and this is achieved by the use of dummies. This, the second stage, is very important and cannot be practised too often ; it develops the enterprise which has already been encouraged, a sense of distance which is so essential to hand-to-hand fighting, and, especially when carried out on rough ground, good balance.

The third stage is that of the training stick, the method o using which, like that of dummies, is described in Pamphlet No. 12 of the " Small Arms Training Manual," Volume I. With the judicious use of this stick, accuracy and speed can be developed to a very high degree of proficiency.

But one thing is still lacking. The pupil, as we may now call him, has not yet faced an opponent armed with the same weapon and trained in the use of it ; nor has he learnt much about defence, and consequently he has neither complete confidence in himself nor the experience of actual combat.

Bayonet Fencing, the fourth and final stage, is an essential, though unfortunately an often neglected, part of the training. Bayonet Fencing gives experience of actual combat against a man similarly armed and trained ; it encourages initiative and self-reliance ; it compels a good defence. A prize-fighter does not enter the ring trained only on shadow boxing and the punch ball.

When training for battle, it might be well to modify to some extent the conventions of Bayonet Fencing. For instance, shouting should be encouraged instead of being penalized ; no attempt should be made (except, perhaps, in the early stages) to have an arena with a flat surface and without obstacles ; butt strokes might sometimes be allowed amongst experienced fencers who are capable of controlling the force of their blows. Tripping might also be allowed in a " corps-à-corps," though every effort should be made to keep the play at a proper distance.

Individuality should not be discouraged and the various types of temperament and physique must be allowed for. Energetic and rapid movements, and attacks pushed well home, combined with ease and harmony of action, are essential for success. Trepidation is the bayonet-fighter's worst enemy, whereas the man who is imbued with a veritable " Bayonet Spirit " will terrify his opponent by his ferocious onslaught and will overcome him by fear before striking a blow. This " Bayonet Spirit," combined with a sound training in the scientific use of the weapon, must be inspired in every man who may be called upon to use a rifle and bayonet, pike, or other such implement of war, either in offence or defence.

Bayonet Fencing, apart from its value in training and practice for Bayonet Fighting, should also be encouraged as a recreation. Both individual and team competitions can be organized, and some notes on the rules for such competitions are given in the Appendices.

The Two Weapons

It is not necessary here to describe the rifle and bayonet, but a short comparison between them and their fencing counterparts may be of interest (see Fig. 1).

The length of the rifle is 3 ft. $8\frac{1}{2}$ in., or 5 ft. $1\frac{1}{4}$ in. with a bayonet fixed; the length of the dummy rifle is 3 ft. 10 in., or 5 ft. 3 in. if the spring-bayonet is included.

The centre of balance of the rifle without the bayonet is 1 ft. 8 in. from the heel of the butt, or 1 ft. 11 in. when the bayonet is fixed; that of the dummy and spring-bayonet is 2 ft. from the same point.

The weight of the rifle alone is 8 lb. $10\frac{1}{2}$ oz., but with the bayonet 9 lb. 12 oz.; the weight of the dummy rifle and spring-bayonet is 9 lb. 4 oz.

A

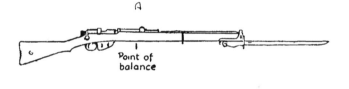

Point of
balance

B

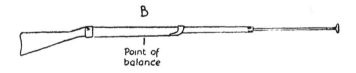

Point of
balance

C

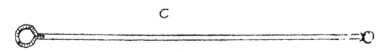

Fig. 1.
A—Rifle and Bayonet.　B—Dummy Rifle.　C—Training Stick.

3

The Fencing Weapon

Bayonet fencing is bayonet fighting practice with a dummy rifle against an opponent similarly armed.

The dummy rifle is fashioned in the manner of a real one; that is to say, it has a steel barrel supported by a wooden stock which is carried beyond the rear end of the barrel to form the butt; the stock, however, is only taken in the direction of the muzzle as far as the band. The spur on the underside of the butt is not reproduced on the dummy, which is a pity as a better grip is given to the right hand when two or three fingers are placed behind this spur.

The bayonet, which is tubular, fits easily into the barrel and is prevented from sliding right out by a milled collar which is screwed into the muzzle; before fencing, it is wise to make sure that this collar is screwed up tightly. Inside the barrel is a spring which bears up against a collar fixed to the end of the bayonet and forces it out until this collar bears up against the milled collar of the muzzle. It is very necessary to keep the bayonet greased in order to prevent it from jamming if a thrust is made slightly out of line with the barrel.

Screwed into the outer end of the bayonet is a knob, called the Button, and this takes the place of the point for fencing purposes and allows a thrust to be made without fear of any damage being done to the opponent. Before fencing, besides confirming that the milled collar is well screwed home, see that this button is firm and that the bayonet slides in and out freely.

Dress for Fencing

Regulation outfits are supplied to the Services. They consist of helmets, padded jackets (which cover the whole of the trunk and arms), and padded gloves, those for the left hand being exceptionally stout. Either long or short trousers can be worn, and underclothing should be light and absorbent as bayonet fencing is hot work. Boots should always be worn except for practice on wooden surfaces, when rubber-soled shoes are preferable. The helmets are heavy and hot to work in, but a handkerchief tied round the head or face before putting the helmet on may be found beneficial.

As it is advisable to take a shower bath after fencing, or at any rate to have a rub down, a towel should also be included in the outfit.

4

The Training Stick

This stick can easily be improvised. Take a light wooden stick 5 ft. 2 in. in length and to one end fasten a stuffed canvas pad, 2 in. in diameter, by wiring it on ; a shallow groove cut round the stick near the end will enable the wiring to secure the pad in place. At the other end of the stick fix a 3-in. wire ring, which must be covered with string or adhesive tape.

The padded end represents the point of a bayonet ; the ring, when presented, a target to be thrust at.

Method of using the Training Stick

The stick can be used by an instructor, in which case he will form his squad round him in a circle and exercise each man in turn. The squad will be armed with their rifles, the bayonets of which are fixed ; but the scabbards must be on, and firmly secured in place by string. This is the best way of carrying out stick training with beginners, but advanced pupils may work in pairs, one with the stick and the other with his rifle, bayonet fixed and scabbard tied on, as described above.

Instructor and pupil come on guard facing each other. As soon as the ring of the stick is presented, the pupil points at it vigorously in an attempt to thrust his bayonet into it, and for this reason the ring must be moved into position quickly and decisively, and held there until the thrust has been made.

To commence with, the instructor holds the stick in the " On Guard " position, right hand about 12 in. from the ring. To present the ring, he draws his left hand back close to the body, but just to the left of it, waist high. At the same time he places the ring in the required position, clear of the body, and turns his head and eyes towards it. When presenting it on his left side he must take a step backwards with his left foot. Points must be made immediately the ring is presented, and with energy.

Wall Pad

Another method of training for accuracy and distance is by the wall pad. Chalk the outline of a man on a board and fill in three bullseyes : one at the centre of the face, one at the centre of the chest, and one at the centre of the abdomen. Fix this board vertically, and the various methods of thrusting, with and without advancing, can be practised at the bullseyes from varying distances, using a spring bayonet. It is better, but not essential, to pad the target in order to absorb some of the shock.

Dummies

A more realistic manner of carrying out thrusting practice is by making use of a dummy, which can easily be manufactured by filling a sack with straw or fine shavings, marking in the three bullseyes, and securing it vertically, at the right height, by the four corners. Against a dummy the real weapon can be used, but after a successful thrust the bayonet must be withdrawn clear of the dummy. Two points in rapid succession can also be practised, or more than one dummy may be used, the dummies being placed at varying distances from one another. In this case the rifle must be carried at the " High Port " when proceeding from one dummy to the next.

NOTE TO INSTRUCTORS

The instructions which follow are set out in a progressive sequence, but divided into chapters at convenient points. Some of the strokes and parries can be first taught in classes or squads who may use real weapons with the bayonets covered. If there is sufficient fencing equipment, however, the best method is, after having given them instruction in one or two of the moves, to place them in pairs facing one another (armed with dummy rifles and dressed for fencing) and let them practise the moves just taught in their own time ; they will then see for themselves the actual value of the movements when made incorrectly and correctly, and the reactions of an opponent.

With a rifle and bayonet appreciably shorter tha nthe one shown on page 3, although the method of handling it is essentially the same as that described in the following pages, an appreciation of the relatively shorter reach will be required, especially when in action against a longer weapon ; the closer fighting distance will tend to increase the value of butt strokes.

6

CHAPTER II

The Guard

A Guard is a position assumed when one is prepared to either attack or defend. The Guard position normally used is taken in the following manner :

From the position of " Attention," turn half-right and advance the left foot about twice its own length in the direction of the opponent, bending both knees in so doing. At the same time cant the rifle forward and seize it with the left hand at the band and with the right hand at the small of the butt, placing two or three fingers over the spur (if there is one) ; the butt should be held close to the body and well forward, the right forearm lying along it. The left arm should be almost straight, with the back of the hand towards the ground.

The body should be erect and evenly balanced over both legs ; cramped and crouching positions must be avoided, but instructors must be careful not to attempt to turn out all their pupils in a set style, allowing positions to be as easy and as natural as possible.

Fig. 2.—On Guard.

The left foot should point towards the opponent (this is important) and the right foot at right angles to it ; it is, nevertheless, better for the right foot to be pointing slightly forward than turned out too far.

Head and eyes will, of course, be turned towards the opponent.

Rest

To rest, drop the butt of the rifle to the ground between the feet and straighten the knees.

Resting Guard

This Guard may be assumed when there is a lull in the fighting or when the opponent is not close enough to attempt a thrust.

From the " On Guard " position described above, lower the left hand and rest it on the left knee ; the right hand may also be lowered.

High Port

This position, which is not used in bayonet fencing, is suitable for close formation, when running, and for encountering obstacles, when the right hand can be freed. From the Guard position, keeping the right elbow close to the side and the right forearm horizontal, draw the left hand backward and upward until the forearm is vertical. The point must be kept well up but pointing diagonally to the left, the rifle held close to the body with the barrel to the rear. At the same time straighten the knees and bring the right foot up to the left foot.

Attack

The bayonet is principally a weapon of attack. A determined and rapid attack, pushed well home, has a good chance of success ; even should it be parried, the very determination and energy with which it is delivered may so upset the opponent that he is unable to make a suitable action in return. A half-hearted attack, on the other hand, is dangerous only to the attacker.

The three parts of the weapon which can be used for attack are the point of the bayonet, the sharp edge of the bayonet, and the butt of the rifle. Attacks with the point, however, are by far the most deadly as well as the most rapid ; they are also the only ones used in bayonet fencing.

Fig. 3.—High Port.

Thrusts

Attacks with the point, called " Thrusts " or " Points," can be made at three levels : the head, the chest (called the " High line "), and the abdomen (called the " Low line "). Every thrust must be made sharply without any drawing back of the weapon beforehand (except in the case of the Short Point), but the bayonet must never be pushed right home. In other words, two or three inches of penetration with the real bayonet (or the spring half compressed with the dummy) is a good thrust. After a successful thrust the rifle must be drawn straight back at once and at least far enough for the point (or button) to be clear of the target ; this process of clearing the point is called the " Withdraw." If, on the other hand, the thrust is unsuccessful, the Guard position should be resumed immediately, or such other position as may be expedient for the continuation of the fight.

9

Target

That part of the opponent on which hits count in Bayonet Fencing is called the " Target " ; it includes the whole of the trunk above the line of the hips, the head, both arms, and either hand if it is not grasping the rifle. Hits which are made correctly but arrive on parts of the opponent other than these are still hits, but do not score.

Hits

In Bayonet Fencing, a hit is a Point delivered cleanly, in the line of the rifle, with a force sufficient to have inflicted a wound on a body unprotected by clothing if the real weapon were being used. A " valid hit " is one which arrives on the Target.

First Point

When on guard, the point should be directed towards the opponent's throat. To make the First Point, first direct the point to the centre of that part of the Target which you intend to hit (the head, high or low line) and straighten the left arm, keeping the butt close to the body and the right forearm against the butt, but now rather on the outside of it instead of on top of it. Then, bracing the right knee smartly, throw the body forward, carrying the rifle with it, as far as possible without losing the balance. It is imperative that the left arm be straight and stiff when making a thrust, and this must be insisted on. The right foot should remain flat on the ground, but if the guard is taken with the toe of the right foot pointing slightly forwards it will not matter if the heel is very slightly raised in making the Point ; but it is important to ensure that the right foot is not allowed to fall over on the inside.

Having made the Point, if successful, withdraw and then come on guard, not forgetting to bend the right knee in so doing ; do not first straighten the knees and then bend them again. If unsuccessful, return on guard straight away without withdrawing, or act in the way you consider most propitious under the circumstances.

When practising thrusts without an opponent, some of them should be with the Withdraw and some without it.

First Point, lunging

In order to increase the reach of the thrust and to preserve a better balance, the First Point can be accompanied by a lunge. This is done by carrying the left foot forward about

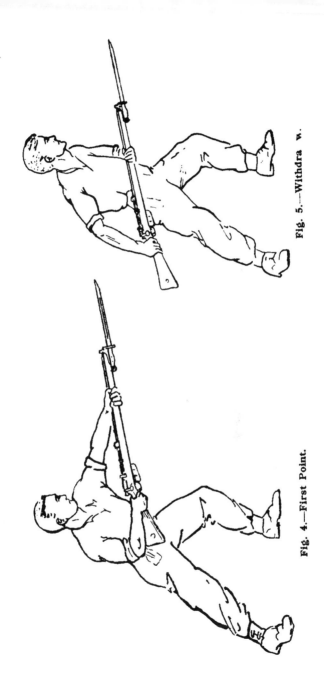

Fig. 4.—First Point.

Fig. 5.—Withdraw.

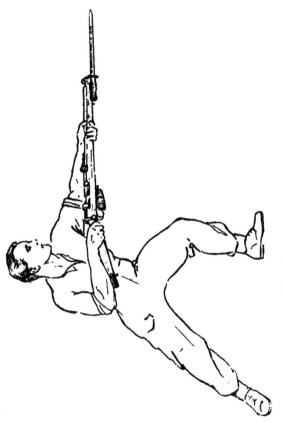

Fig. 6.—First Point, Lunging.

its own length and bending the knee a little more at the same time as the right knee is braced.

Recovery

The Recovery, or the return on guard, should follow as soon as possible after the lunge (but not before the withdraw), as the lunge is a difficult position from which to manœuvre. It is a similar movement to the return on guard from the First Point without lunge, except that the left foot is brought back as the right knee is bent; the same observation with regard to not straightening the knees applies.

Advance

If the distance from your opponent is too great for you to make a First Point, with or without a lunge, you can close it by advancing. This is a simple movement, but one that is often spoilt by a straightening of one or both knees. Both knees must remain bent. Move the left foot forward the required distance and then bring the right foot forward exactly the same distance.

Retire

If you are too close to your opponent, or if he advances upon you, move the right foot back the required distance and follow this by an equal movement backward of the left foot; here again the observation with regard to keeping the knees bent must be insisted upon.

First Point, advancing

Instead of lunging with your First Point you can advance with it. As you straighten your left arm, step forward with the left foot; bring the right foot forward the same distance and straighten the right knee.

Advance and First Point, lunging

This attack consists of an Advance followed immediately by a First Point, lunging. A good deal of ground is covered, but the feet must move very rapidly (left, right, left) and in harmony with the body or the balance will suffer. Aim is taken on the first movement of the Advance, the left arm is straightened on the second, and, of course, the thrust itself is made on the third.

13

CHAPTER III

Defence

As the bayonet is principally a weapon of attack, it is possible that your opponent will attempt to attack you before you are able to attack him. It is therefore necessary for you to know how to defend yourself, the most usual way of doing which is by parrying.

Parries

To parry is to knock or guide your opponent's rifle out of line as he attacks. A Parry must be neither too late nor too early, because if it is too late the attack will arrive and the Parry will not then be required ; if it is too early, either your rifle will have moved too far when the attack does come in, and will thus miss the opponent's weapon, or he will notice your movement and will attack somewhere else instead, or not attack at all.

On the other hand, if you judge his movement correctly and adjust yours to it you will prevent him from hitting you.

Parries should never be made with the bayonet itself, nor with the barrel of the rifle, as either this or the sights may become damaged, and it must not be forgotten that the rifle may be required for shooting purposes at any time. Therefore, always parry with the stock ; that is to say, in such a way that the stock takes the blow.

Parries may be made on the retire, but unless the opponent's attack is of such a nature that it renders the retire necessary it is better not to do so. It is also permissible to retire without parrying on an attack, but, except in certain cases such as when you are decoying an opponent, this should not be encouraged as it tends to give him confidence.

Right Parry

When on guard your bayonet is pointing slightly to the left of the centre line and, the opponent being in the same guard, his point will be to the right of yours ; that is to say, inside yours, and his most direct attack will therefore be on the inside. As he makes his thrust in this line, straighten the left arm smartly, tighten the grip of the right hand and, turning the stock of your rifle slightly to the right, knock his point sharply

14

Fig. 7.—Right Parry.

away to the right. You must knock his weapon directly to the right, keeping your own point up; this is very important. A beginner must watch for the following errors : Not straightening the left arm ; lowering the point ; allowing your rifle to move further to the right than is absolutely necessary to cover yourself ; knocking his weapon downward (which will only push him from the high line to the low and will most probably not prevent you being hit even if not in the way your opponent intended) ; swaying the body forward as the parry is made.

15

Left Parry

Should the opponent attack you outside your weapon—that is to say, to the left of it—push the butt forward without raising it until it is almost in front of the left hip, tightening the grasp of the right hand and turning the stock slightly to the left; at the same time smartly straighten the left arm and carry the point directly to the left, keeping the point up.   Observations similar to those mentioned above apply to this parry also.

Fig. 8.—Left Parry.

The Return

If you parry correctly you will foil your opponent's attack and for the moment he will be nonplussed; his mind will have been concentrated on attack and not on defence, and you will have a wonderful opportunity of counter-attacking him, provided you act without delay.   A Parry, therefore, should be not only a position or a movement which prevents the opponent from hitting you, but also one from which a counter-attack can readily and rapidly be launched.

If you beat off your opponent's attack with a properly formed Parry, moreover, you open a line for your counter-attack. This counter-attack is called the " Return " or " Riposte."

He will obviously try to close the line as soon as possible, but if you return immediately after a well-formed Parry you are fairly certain of hitting him. If you parry badly, however, there is little chance of doing so. The Parry and the Return must both be definite movements, though there should be no interval of time between them even if the Return is made in a different line from the Parry.

Fig. 9.—Low Left Parry.

Low Left Parry

If instead of attacking you on the outside over your left arm your opponent attacks under your left arm, tighten the grip of the right hand and, smartly straightening your left arm, throw the muzzle of your rifle downward and slightly to the left. Take care not to let your point go farther to the left than is absolutely necessary or you will have difficulty in making your Return ; do not raise the right hand or shoulder, and do not sway the body.

The Gain

To gain, bring the right foot up to the left foot and then carry the left foot forward an equal distance, keeping the knees bent all the time.

This movement can be used in place of the Advance for gaining ground, but although you move forward rather more than in the Advance, there is a momentary weakness in your balance when both feet are close together, and on rough ground there is a much greater chance of tripping over a large tuft of grass, a small rock, or some such obstacle, when moving the left foot forward. (The same observation applies equally well to a movement to the rear made in a similar way ; that is to say, by moving the forward foot first.)

The Long Lunge

This is a combination of the Gain and the Lunge when you wish to attack from rather far off. Keeping the knees bent, bring the right foot up to the left foot and then, by bracing the right knee, push the body forward and carry the left foot to the lunge position.

Traversing

In Bayonet Fencing, as in Bayonet Fighting, there is no reason why you should not move round your opponent, and the movement to employ is the Traverse. It can be either to the right or to the left ; in the first case the right foot moves first, in the second the left foot, both knees remaining bent throughout the movement.

CHAPTER IV

The Beat

If your opponent is well covered you will probably wish to "create an opening," and one way of doing this is by making use of the Beat.

A Beat is made in a manner somewhat like a Parry, but on a point which is not extended, and it must be followed immediately by a thrust. Its efficacy is largely dependent upon its suddenness and its sharpness. It need not be heavy—in fact, it is better when not so—but it must be unexpected and therefore there must be no drawing away of the rifle just beforehand for the purpose of giving a heavier blow.

The Beat is a preparation for an attack and must not be separated from it or it loses its value ; it is of no use by itself. Continued tappings of the weapons which some beginners make are not beats and are quite useless ; they neither frighten nor annoy the opponent.

Inside Beat

If you are engaged on the inside, your weapon may or may not be touching that of the opponent. If the bayonets are crossing but not touching, the Inside Beat will be made in exactly the same way as the Right Parry. If the bayonets are not touching on account of being out of distance, the Beat will be made in the same way, but will be accompanied by an advance. If the bayonets are crossing and touching, the Beat becomes far more difficult because, as mentioned above, there must be no draw back ; that is to say, no appreciable draw back. The Beat must knock the other weapon aside, it must not push it, therefore the sharpness can only be given by smartly tightening the grip of the right hand as the left arm throws the rifle to the right ; the stock must, as in the Parry, be turned slightly towards the opponent's weapon. Immediately after the blow your own point must be brought into line for the thrust while the opponent's weapon is still out of line. The beginner will require a great deal of practice to get a smart, sharp and sudden Beat.

Outside Beat

This, being a back-handed movement, is far more difficult to make than the Inside Beat, and is less like the Left Parry than the Inside Beat is like the Right Parry.

In the first place, the right hand is not pushed forward; it remains where it is, but it grips the rifle more tightly and gives the slight but necessary turn to protect the sights.

In the second place, the left arm is not straightened till after the beat, the rifle being pulled to the left with the arm still slightly bent. It is, moreover, impossible to make this beat from contact without a draw back; therefore it should not be attempted from this position. The same observations apply with regard to bringing the point into line before the opponent can do so, and to the shortness, suddenness and sharpness of the blow.

In both these beats the point must be kept up until the beat has contacted the other weapon; it is far too risky to beat with a horizontal weapon, when there is every chance of beating nothing but air.

Beat by Change

It is not necessary to make the beat in the line in which you are engaged; you can make a Beat by Change, that is to say, by dipping your point under the opposing weapon and beating on the other side. This beat made with a change of line must be carried out in one movement only, and in doing so your point must pass as close as possible to the opponent's rifle. You must not draw your point backward, but rather move it forward in making the change.

Defence against the Beat

There are two ways in which you can deal with a Beat; you can resist it or you can avoid it, but in either case you have to think and act quickly, instinctively. The more natural way is to counter force by force; that is to say, beat by a similar beat in the same line but in the opposite direction. The less obvious way is by removing your weapon out of the way so that the beat beats nothing. To do this, which by the way is usually unexpected by your opponent, you simply drop the point of your bayonet just as he makes his beat, so that his weapon passes over the top of yours and, not meeting with the resistance expected, it goes wider than intended, giving you time to extend your weapon and thrust. To avoid in this manner requires a very quick brain, and it is almost necessary to sense the beat before it is made ; it therefore requires much practice and experience.

Disengagement

If the line in which you find yourself is very firmly closed, and for some reason you do not wish to try to open it with a beat, you can disengage, for the other line must, in consequence, be open.

To do this, as you make your thrust, dip the point under the other rifle and come in on the other side. This movement differs from the Change in that you completely straighten the left arm and throw the body forward as your point comes round into the new line, whereas in the Change the left arm does not straighten and the body remains stationary. A Disengagement is made in one movement only ; if you were first to Change and then Thrust you would make the attack in two movements, and this would be a Change and Point.

Feint

To feint is to make a movement which resembles an attack, but with which you do not intend to obtain a hit, in order to draw the opponent away from the line in which you actually mean to strike. It must be really convincing, but will naturally vary according to the temperament and sensitiveness of the opponent ; a highly strung fencer answers to a very slight Feint, while a phlegmatic fencer may require one which all but hits.

The attack proper should follow immediately after the Feint.

Feint Point and Disengage

Feint a thrust in the line in which the bayonets are crossed and, as your opponent parries, dip your point under and thrust in the opposite line. In doing this, you must be careful to fit the disengagement in with his parry, and you should not meet his weapon. If you are too slow you will find he has parried you ; if you are too fast he may not have reacted to the feint and you will make your true attack in a closed line instead of in an open one.

One-Two

This is also a Feint and a Thrust, but the feint is not in the original line but in the opposite one, and the true thrust is made by returning into the original line ; in other words, it consists of two disengagements, the second following immediately on top of the first, hence the name. The timing of this is important as you must move round to the second disengagement as the opponent is making his parry, and you must make the final thrust before he has time to move back again. The point of the bayonet should be moving forward throughout the whole attack, the left arm straightening on the first disengagement and the body thrown forward, with or without a lunge as the case may be, on the second.

Beat and Disengage

As before, the Beat is the preparation for the attack. You know that if your opponent's reaction to your beat is to oppose it he will close that line quickly, but in doing so will open the other, and therefore, instead of making a Beat and Point where you risk strong opposition, you follow up your beat with a thrust in the other, the open, line.

In this case it is not so important to conceal the beat ; in fact, it may be wise to pronounce it by slightly drawing your weapon away a little first, but you must not do so to such an extent that he may either suspect a trap or thrust quickly in an open line.

Half-Disengagement

So far we have dealt only with Disengagements in the high line, but it is quite possible to go from the high line to the low —or *vice versa*—instead of from one side of the opposing weapon to the other.

The Half-Disengage can rarely be used by itself on the inside, but it can on the outside ; nevertheless, it can be used in either line in conjunction with one or more other movements. For instance, you can make a Right Beat and Half-Disengage, or a Beat by Change outside and Half-Disengage. You can Disengage outside, to draw a Left Parry, and Half-Disengage below ; or Half-Disengage below to draw a low parry, and Half-Disengage again into the high line.

But before attempting these attacks test your opponent's reactions to beats and disengagements.

Circular Parry

If you are engaged on the inside and your opponent disengages outside, the simplest defence is the Left Parry. But if you always make the simplest moves the opponent will soon realize this fact and, if he is an experienced fencer, he will know exactly what to do to defeat you. It is therefore necessary to be able to vary your play, and in the case in question, instead of parrying left, follow his point round and make a Right Parry instead ; your opponent will thus find himself back in the line from which he started instead of the opposite line which he expected, and your Circular Parry will embarrass him.

Centre Parry

This parry is seldom used in Bayonet Fencing as the only really practical return is with the butt. However, in an emergency it can be used, even in fencing, by itself.

Fig. 10.—Centre Parry.

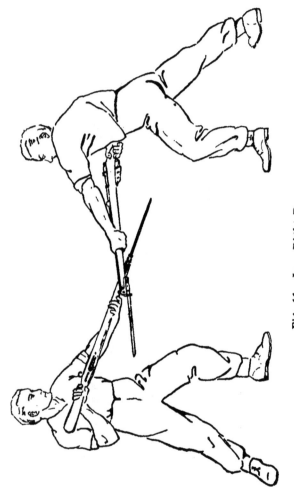

Fig. 11.—Low Right Parry.

As the opponent thrusts in the low line, raise the rifle to a vertical position in front of, and just outside, the left knee by drawing back the left hand towards the left shoulder, at the same time pushing the right hand downward to the left front, to a position just above the left knee, taking care not to drop the left shoulder.

The opposing weapon is warded off with that part of the rifle which lies between the hands.

Low Right Parry

Like the Centre Parry, this is seldom used in Bayonet Fencing. Its principal use is against an attack at the legs, although it can be made after a Left Parry against an attack by Point outside and Half-Disengage.

From your Left Parry, drop the point and carry it across to the right, at the same time raising the right hand to a position near the right breast. The butt must come up on the far side of the forearm and the rifle should be turned to take the parry with the stock. The slope of the rifle should be about 45 degrees, with the rifle lying in a plane parallel to the Directing Line. (The Directing Line is an imaginary straight line joining your left foot to that of the opponent.)

Compound Returns

It will be seen that a Parry-and-Return is almost the same as a Counter-attack by Beat and Point on the opponent's thrust ; a Parry and Return by Disengagement is almost the same as a Counter-attack·on the opponent's thrust, by Beat and Disengage. The Return, moreover, can take the form of any compound attack, such as the Feint Point and Disengage, etc. The Return used will, of course, depend on the opponent's play, but, generally speaking, the simpler the better.

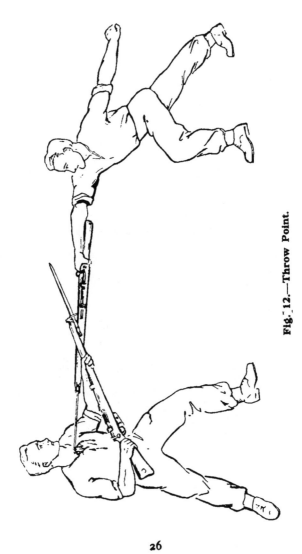

Fig. 12.—Throw Point.

CHAPTER V

Throw Point

This is a most useful thrust in Fencing ; it can also be used in Fighting ; but in either case it must only be used when you are confident of hitting with it, as if you fail to hit you are left in a precarious position unless you have the recovery well in hand. It must be made immediately the opportunity arises and with the utmost speed and suddenness.

Throw the point forward on to the target to the full extent of the right arm and brace the right knee. The rifle must be horizontal, or with the point slightly higher than the hand, at the moment of impact ; this thrust is never aimed at the low line. In order to preserve the balance, as the left hand releases its grasp of the rifle the left arm must be thrown to the rear, and to keep the point up it is better to turn the barrel to the left so that the butt rests against the under side of the right forearm.

A longer reach is obtained with the Throw than with the First Point, even if the First Point is taken with a lunge, but great care should be taken not to " plunge," that is to say, not to raise the hand and allow the point to move through the arc of a circle and arrive in a downward direction. The thrust must be shot forward in a straight line, whether made at the high line or at the head.

If a hit is scored by the Throw with a sharp weapon, the Withdraw is made by pulling backward sharply with the right hand after having given a slight twist to the rifle ; at the same time the left hand must be thrown forward and a normal grasp retaken.

If a hit is scored with the dummy rifle this recovery is unnecessary, but should be practised.

On failing to score a hit (with either weapon) by means of the Throw, it is most important to recover quickly both on account of the weight of the weapon and for defensive purposes ; also because, until you have recovered, further attack is out of the question. This is done in the same manner as the Withdraw, although the twist of the rifle is unnecessary.

There is a certain " swing " about this thrust and a quick recovery which makes the latter quite easy ; a fraction of delay, however, seems to add pounds of weight to the point and it will drop before the left hand can regain its grasp.

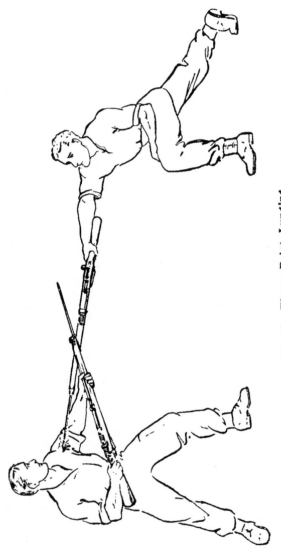

Fig. 13.—Throw Point, Lunging.

28

Throw, lunging

With a lunge, the reach of the Throw is greatly increased, so is the force. And by placing the left forearm on the left leg, just above the knee, instead of throwing it backward, the left hand can be taken off the rifle a fraction of a second later (because it has not so far to travel) and can be returned a fraction of a second earlier; and while the left arm is free there is support being given by the left arm in conjunction with the left leg so that the rifle appears to have less weight than when the left arm is thrown back. This, of course, applies only to the Throw, lunging.

Passing

To pass is to carry the rear foot forward and place it on the ground in front of the other foot, or *vice versa*. When no direction—forward or backward—is mentioned in conjunction with the Pass it is assumed that the Pass is forward. The distance the foot is moved depends upon the particular circumstances, but usually it is as far as is comfortably possible.

Throw, passing

The reach which can be gained with the Throw, passing, is remarkable. As you make your Throw, pass the right foot as far forward as possible, swinging round on the left toe, throwing the right shoulder forward and the left arm backward.

When withdrawing or recovering from this thrust, swing the left arm forward and the right shoulder backward; at the same time pass backward and jerk the rifle back into the left hand which comes forward to meet it. This is the only point which should be made with the right foot forward.

Extra Parry

Supposing that for some reason or other you fail to recover from your Throw and the point of your rifle drops to the ground. You will, of course, try to regain control of it at once, but if the opponent is too smart for you he will attack without giving you such an opportunity; you will then have to protect yourself as best you can; that is to say, with the Extra Parry.

Leaving the point on the ground, raise the right hand until the rifle is almost vertical, with the barrel to the rear. Guard

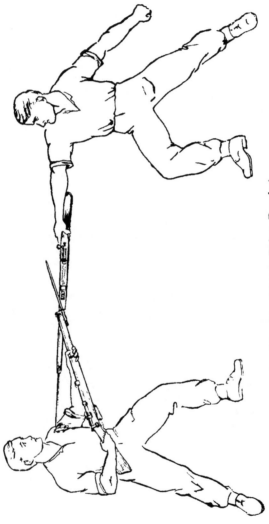

Fig. 14.—Throw Point, Passing.

Fig. 15.—Extra Parry.

yourself by moving the butt to the right or to the left as the case may be, retiring all the while, until such time as you can jerk the rifle into the guard position.

This Parry can only be regarded as a *faute de mieux* ; nevertheless it can save defeat, although there is, of course, no possible Return.

Re-attack

Should your opponent retire on your attack, with or without parrying, you can attack him again immediately by Gaining. When by means of the Gain you go from one lunge to another without coming to the normal guard stance on the way, you Re-attack, and the distance covered is considerable.

Jump

This movement is sometimes called the Double Jump, and has for its object the losing of ground hurriedly after a lunge. Being in the lunge position, leap backward as far as possible, pushing off with the left foot, and assume the guard stance.

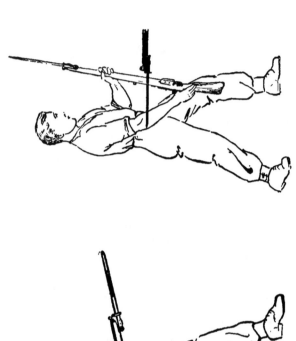

Fig. 17.—Right Centre Parry.

Fig. 16.—Shorten Arms.

Short Point

If you find that you are too close to the opponent to make a First Point, but not quite close enough to be able to touch him with your hand (a position which should be avoided if possible), you can make a Short Point. But first you must shorten arms by drawing the rifle straight to the rear until the left forearm is touching the body ; at the same time lean slightly backward, well bend the right knee and straighten the left knee. Then throw the point forward to the full extent of the left arm, swinging the body forward by straightening the right knee and bending the left knee.

To withdraw, pull the rifle sharply backward and assume the Shorten Arms position again.

Parrying the Short Point

You will only be able to parry the Short Point with an ordinary parry if you can either jump or step back with it ; moreover, you will have to time both your parry and the backward movement very carefully indeed.

If you do not move backward you will have to make use of either a Centre Parry or a Right Centre Parry according to which side of your rifle the opponent makes his thrust. The Right Centre Parry is made in a manner similar to that of the Centre (or Left Centre) Parry with the exception that the rifle is held vertically on the right side of the body and the stock is turned slightly to the right.

The best return from a Centre Parry is with the butt, but as the use of this part of the rifle is disallowed in Bayonet Fencing, you must either return with a Short Point or jump clear.

After the Right Centre Parry, the Short Point is quick, but it is necessary to maintain the same distance ; that is to say, you must not allow the opponent to either open or close it.

Close Up

When you are so close to your opponent that you can touch him with your hand, the distance is " Close Up " and you should adopt a Close Up Guard.

In a Close Up Guard the right elbow must be close against the right side and the forearm horizontal. The left hand, still holding the rifle at the band, should be lower than in the High

Fig. 18.—Close Up Guards (Left and Right).

Port, so that the rifle is pointing upwards and to the left at an angle of about 45 degrees or a little nearer to the horizontal ; the barrel of the rifle should be to the rear.

Right Close Up Guard

In the Right Close Up Guard the right leg is forward with the knee bent ; the left knee should be almost straight, but the stance should not be wide and, although the weight of the body is over the right knee, the body must be held in an upright position.

Left Close Up Guard

This Guard is similar in all respects to the above with the sole exception that the left foot is forward, the left knee bent and the right knee almost straight.

Close Up Fighting

To use the point in a Close Up is impossible. In a fight with sharp weapons, butt strokes and tripping would normally take the place of thrusts, although kicking, the use of the knee and other unsportsmanlike tricks would not be out of place.

In Bayonet Fencing, however, these are all forbidden. Taking hold of the opponent's weapon is permitted, provided neither the point nor the edge of the bayonet is touched—a rule which also applies to parries made with the hand. But whether parrying or seizing with the hand, the following point must not be lost sight of : you cannot manœuvre the rifle with one hand alone.

In Bayonet Fencing, therefore, before you can attempt to hit it is essential that you get away from your opponent, and in doing so you lay yourself open to be hit. Your getaway must consequently be as unexpected and as instantaneous as possible. You can step or pass backward to the Shorten Arms position and make a Short Point, not forgetting that, if the opponent senses your move, he can also make a Short Point ; or he can parry. Otherwise you must Break, remembering that here also the opponent can Shorten Arms, or he can attack before you have recovered from the violence of your movement.

Breaking

Assuming that your opponent is also in a Close Up Guard, the rifles will be crossed middle to middle and touching. Choosing the moment warily, jump to the rear as far as possible, assuming the guard position, or parrying if he thrusts. You might be able to attack immediately afterwards, but this is not usually advisable as you are not likely to see an opening during your Break, and if you get clear successfully you have time to develop a less hazardous operation.

As you break, by pressing your rifle against the opponent's for as long as possible (that is to say, until your arms are straight) you will not only give added force to your break, but you will prevent him moving his rifle as soon as he might otherwise do. If you do not choose the right moment for breaking and your opponent is therefore not taken by surprise, he will probably stab at you as you go back; it is under these circumstances that your parry will be required.

CHAPTER VI

Action in Time

Broadly speaking, Action in Time—or " Timing," as it is often called—is the making of a counter-attack at the same time as the opponent either attacks or prepares to attack, being aware that he is taking, or is about to take, the offensive.

Simultaneous Action

This action, which must not be confused with Action in Time, arises from the simultaneous initiation of attacks by the two fencers, each being ignorant of the other's intention.

Time Thrust

A Time Thrust, which is an Action in Time, is a thrust made on the opponent's attack in such a way that it either parries the final movement of his attack or prevents this movement from being made by barring its way.

Attack on the Preparation

This is an attack made as the opponent prepares to make his attack. In Bayonet Fencing, attacks are seldom of a very complicated nature, so that Attacks on the Preparation, other than the Stop Thrust, are seldom possible.

Stop Thrust

A thrust made " in time " on an opponent as he moves forward either with a bent arm or with his point wide of the target is a Stop Thrust.

Back Lunge

Any Action in Time, but especially a Stop Thrust, may be made with a Back Lunge ; that is to say, as you make your counter-attack, assume the usual lunge position by carrying the right foot backward instead of moving the left foot forward.

Under Stop Thrust

A Throw Point used as a Stop Thrust in conjunction with an extended Back Lunge is called an " Under Stop Thrust " because, in this stroke, the body is lowered to such an extent that the opponent's bayonet may well pass overhead. The Throw will, of course, be made in an upward direction, and it is not necessary to turn the back of the right hand upward. An exaggerated form of this Stop Thrust is made by dropping the body forward on to the left knee and, if necessary, putting the left hand on the ground ; in other words, by " avoiding " low. This is, however, only an emergency stroke, and is for experienced fighters only.

Avoiding

Instead of defending yourself by diverting the opponent's attack with your weapon, you can on occasions remove your body out of the way of the thrust ; this action is called " Avoiding."

Generally it is made in conjunction with a thrust or butt stroke, and thus it becomes part of an Action in Time (*e.g.*, the exaggerated Under Stop Thrust). However, it may also be made by lunging to the left front as the opponent thrusts inside, making the preparation for your counter-attack at the same time.

Retiring instead of parrying is also avoiding.

Decoys

A Decoy is a movement which is made in order to deceive the opponent with the idea of getting him to attack in a certain line or manner for which you have some preconceived reply in hand.

False Attack

This must not be confused with the Feint Attack, which is a true attack, one or more movements of which are feints. In making a False Attack you have really no intention of hitting, but it is most essential that it should appear to your opponent that you have. A False Attack may be used as a Decoy, but it may also be used to find out his reactions to a form of attack in a certain line.

Invite

An Invite is one form of a Decoy. For example, you may let your point fall away to the left—apparently unwittingly—in order to entice the opponent to attack high inside; but you are really prepared to parry such an attack and return. You " invite " him to attack you high inside.

Attack of the First Intention

A true attack, with or without preparation, which is made with the intention of hitting.

Attack of the Second Intention

A False Attack made as a Decoy with the intention of drawing an Action in Time from the opponent ; on this Action in Time you are prepared to parry and return.

Attack of the Third Intention

A False Attack made with the intention of drawing a certain parry and return for which you have a parry and return in hand.

Remise

If your opponent parries your attack and fails either to hold the parry or to return, you can continue your attack in the same line without pausing ; this is a Remise.

Redouble

If your opponent parries correctly but does not return, you can redouble your attack in another line, or even in the same line if you can open it by a feint or beat. You also Redouble if you attack again on an opponent who has avoided your first attack by retiring, but in either case the Redouble must follow immediately on the other. One way of Redoubling is by the Re-attack (see page 31).

Fig. 19.—Right Butt Stroke.

CHAPTER VII

The Butt

In battle, the butt of the rifle can sometimes be used to great advantage under conditions which render the use of the point impossible, or at any rate difficult. Nevertheless, the butt seldom deals a fatal blow and consequently must be followed by a bayonet thrust; therefore the use of the butt should only be resorted to when the chance of success with that end of the weapon greatly outweighs the chance of success with the point, and this most usually happens after a parry.

In Bayonet Fencing, Butt Strokes are forbidden, partly to encourage the use of the point, and partly because serious injury can easily be inflicted by them when made at the head. By experienced fencers they can be practised provided the blow is checked before impact. Butt Fencing can also be practised with broomsticks cut to the right length and the ends padded.

Right Butt

This, the most usual Butt Stroke, is made with the toe of the Butt, and is a very good return after a Low Left or Centre Parry, though its use need not be restricted to this.

From the position of the Low Left Parry, bring the left elbow back close to the left side, bending the left arm so that the left hand is in front of the left shoulder; then step well forward with the right foot, swinging the butt of the rifle up and round, and strike the left side of the opponent's head with the toe of the butt in a horizontal plane. The blow should be made rather like a " right hook " in boxing, back of the hand up.

If made from the Centre Parry, the left hand will already be in position.

Should the opponent raise his left arm to cover his face, the blow may be diverted to the left flank, in which case the rifle will not be brought to the horizontal position. But this stroke, Butt at Flank, is more hazardous because there is a possibility of the opponent either dropping his arm and taking the blow on that or, although the blow arrives at the flank, the force of the blow is reduced by another part of the rifle striking the opponent's left arm or shoulder.

41

Fig. 20.—Butt Thrust.

Butt Thrust

Swing the muzzle of the rifle upward and backward over the left shoulder, as far to the rear as possible, with the barrel downward and the rifle horizontal ; at the same time pass forward with the right foot, bending the right knee slightly and bracing the left knee. Keeping the rifle horizontal, drive the butt, end on, straight into the opponent's face.

Butt Thrust, avoiding

As the opponent makes a determined First Point, with or without a lunge, avoid left (that is to say, lunge well to the left front, leaning a little to the left if necessary to avoid his point), bringing the rifle to the preparatory position for a Butt Thrust. In this case the toe of the butt may be either up or to the left. Make your Butt Thrust at face, passing forward.

Should your opponent raise his right arm to protect his face, divert the thrust to his right flank.

42

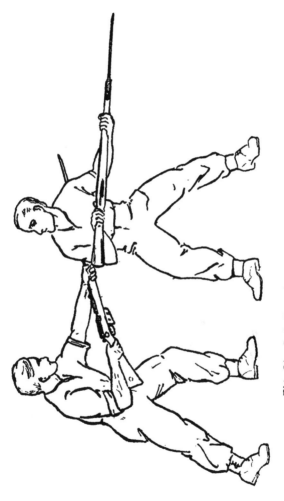

Fig. 21.—Left Butt Stroke (or Butt Thrust, avoiding).

43

Fig. 23.—Left Ankle Trip.

Fig. 22.—Right Ankle Trip.

44

Tripping

When in a Close Up, instead of breaking, using the knee, or using the butt, Tripping can sometimes be employed, although it must be realized that further action will always be necessary after your man is thrown.

A successful trip depends rather on balance and surprise than on strength, the object being to put your opponent in such a position that he cannot retain his balance without moving one of his feet, but this he is prevented from doing by the position in which you have placed yourself; at the same time you must remain well balanced yourself with no fear of being thrown or of falling.

Unless you are both in the same Close Up stance, it is difficult to get into the right position for Tripping.

Right Ankle Trip

If you are both in the Right Close Up guard, take the whole weight of your rifle with the left hand, remove the right hand from the butt and, passing it over your butt and between his left arm and his rifle, place it against his left shoulder. At the same time, pass your right leg outside and behind his, bending the knee slightly and throwing the greater part of your weight on it; lean slightly forward over him. Then press with a circular motion forward, downward and to the left, pulling back with your left hand to force the butt of your rifle into his stomach.

Left Ankle Trip

This is a similar throw made on the other side from the Left Close Up guard, but, on account of the difficulty of holding the rifle in the right hand alone, when placing the left hand on the opponent's right shoulder, allow the rifle to rest on your left forearm.

The Kill

In all probability, when being thrown by an Ankle Trip, your opponent will instinctively remove one hand from his rifle in order to use it for breaking his fall; he may even let go with both hands. In any case he will be more concerned with saving himself than with attacking you, so that as soon as you

Fig. 24.—Kill (following Ankle Trip).

are certain that he cannot recover his balance, step backward (after a Left Ankle Trip) or pass backward (after a Right Ankle Trip), shortening arms as you do so, and thrust immediately where you see a good opening.

You will not be able to decide beforehand at what point to aim as you cannot be quite sure of the way in which he will land on the ground and of the amount of control he will still have of his weapon. You must therefore act on the spur of the moment in the way that appears to be the best under the circumstances. Nevertheless, you must thrust before he has time to recover himself. You must kill, and kill quickly.

The Withdraw

To withdraw, place your left foot on the body, slipping your left hand along the barrel towards the hilt of the bayonet. Then withdraw by pulling with both hands in the direction of the butt and pushing with the left foot.

Unarmed Defence

If, unarmed, you find yourself face to face with an adversary armed with a rifle and bayonet who, for some reason or other, obviously intends to attack you with steel, you must realize that he can only use his weapon, point or butt, when at a convenient distance. You are safe when out of his reach, and you have the advantage of him, even for attack, if you are very close to him ; his weapon is then an encumbrance to him.

To get to this very close range, however, you will have to pass through that stage where you are almost at his mercy, where he can make full use of his point or his butt. You must therefore be armed with a cool head, agility, and the knowledge that the weight of his weapon hinders every sudden movement on his part. You must be prepared to move quickly, either to the right or to the left ; your position, therefore, is square on to him, with the feet apart and knees slightly bent, while the hands must be held ready for immediate action. He may rush at you or he may approach carefully, but in either case he will have his bayonet pointing towards you, and when within striking distance he is almost certain to make his thrust.

Whether you wait for him to thrust or whether you attack him before he does so, your movements will be the same. You must get inside his guard, and the sooner you do so the

Fig. 25.—Withdraw (following Ankle Trip).

better, but the choice of going in on the left side of his bayonet or on the right side will necessitate some very quick thinking on your part. " He who hesitates is lost " must be your motto. If you are quick on your feet you may be able to feint on one side and come in on the other, but this is a very risky thing to do as, if he is not quite as quick-witted as you are, you may throw yourself right in the line of his thrust as you dodge from one side to the other.

Right-Hand Parry

Lunge forward and to the left with the right foot, bending the body over to the left to avoid his point, and at the same time fend off the rifle with the right hand or forearm, but do not grasp the bayonet. Keep your eyes on the opponent all the time.

Right-Hand Counter-attack

1. Pass forward with the left foot, place your left hand on your opponent's right hand and your right hand under his left hand, grasping firmly in order to prevent him loosening his grip.

Fig. 26.—Right-hand Counter-attack (Phase 1).

2. Push vertically downward with the left hand, bringing your left shoulder to a position directly over the hand in order to add your weight to this movement.

3. Pass forward with the right foot, and with the right hand force the barrel of the rifle upward and forward, keeping the elbow as close to the side as possible, and then downward behind the opponent's right shoulder, bringing your own right shoulder forward in order to get the full weight of your body over his right shoulder.

Fig. 27.—Right-hand Counter-attack (Phase 2).

4. Keeping your left arm as straight as possible, force your opponent downward towards your own feet with both your

hands and the full weight of your body, bending both knees in so doing.

NOTE.—The success of this counter-attack chiefly depends on—

(a) Preventing the opponent from releasing his grasp of the rifle ;
(b) Forcing the butt down at the very start ;
(c) Keeping the elbows in ;
(d) Getting the weight of your body well over his right shoulder ;
(e) Forcing him downwards towards your own feet.

Alternative Counter-attacks*

Your opponent's mind will almost certainly be concentrated on his thrust, and it is therefore unlikely that he will be expecting a counter-attack. Nevertheless, you must be prepared for the exceptional case in which he realizes in time that he has missed you and that you are closing with him.

He may do one of three things. He may withdraw his rifle, he may make a Right Butt Stroke, or he may raise his right hand and push down with his left in order to prevent you from disarming him as described above. He will not forget, however, that the rifle belongs to him, and he will hold on to it with all his might. You, on the other hand, have never been in possession of it, and even if you fail to secure it you will be no worse off than you were before.

Counter for the Withdraw

1. Keep close to the opponent and grip his left hand with your right hand, underneath, with the back of the hand towards the ground.

2. Turn your left side to the rifle and place your left hand on his left wrist, gripping tightly.

3. Holding firmly, raise the rifle barrel and pass under it by stepping out with the right foot.

4. Swing round quickly to face the rifle, still gripping tightly, and twist away from you with both hands until he either releases the rifle or falls to the ground.

---

* NOTE.—A short unarmed man, when counter-attacking a tall armed man, may, on account of his size, find it more convenient to use an alternative counter. For additional Counters the student should study " Unarmed Combat."

Fig. 29.—Left-hand Counter-attack
(Phase 2).

Fig. 28.—Left-hand Counter-attack
(Phase 1).

Before carrying out this counter-attack you may have an opportunity of punching his face with your left hand, butting him in the face, or kicking him hard on the shins. Make full use of such an opportunity, holding his left hand with your right hand.

Counter for the Right Butt

1. Parry with the left hand against his right hand or butt and seize his rifle with your hand as above.
2. Carry out the same counter as for the Withdraw, getting your left elbow over his rifle immediately after the parry or kick.

Counter for the Raised Butt

As above, or bring your knee into his fork with as hearty a jab as you can.

Left-Hand Parry

As for the Right-Hand Parry, reading left for right and *vice versa*.

Left-Hand Counter-attack

1. Pass the right foot forward, gripping the opponent's left elbow firmly with the right hand, back of the hand up.
2. Push downward with the right hand and seize the barrel of the rifle just below the bayonet (or his left hand) with your left hand, back of the hand down. During this movement the body must be turned towards the rifle.
3. With the left hand, force the barrel upward and forward (keeping the elbows as close to the sides as possible), and then, swivelling to the right on both feet, force it backward over his left shoulder, pulling him in as close as possible to yourself.
4. Bringing your chest directly over the rifle and as far forward as possible, and pulling him to you, force him down, bending the right knee in so doing. During this action you may find it advantageous to push your left elbow against his throat and thus get an added leverage under his chin.

NOTE.—The success of this counter-attack chiefly depends on—

    (*a*) Keeping him as close to you as possible ;
    (*b*) Keeping your right elbow close to your side ;

Fig. 30.—Kill (following Disarm).

    (c) Keeping your left elbow either gripping the rifle or under his chin ;

    (d) Getting your weight well over him ;

    (e) Pushing with the left elbow.

Counter for the Withdraw

1. Your opponent, if he is prepared for your counter-attack—which is unlikely—will probably withdraw. If he does so, step in and grasp his left hand firmly with both of yours, left hand underneath and right on top.

2. Twist away from you sharply, still gripping tightly with both hands, and thus either disarm or throw him.

The Disarm

As you force your opponent to the ground after either a Right- or Left-Hand Counter-attack, jerk the rifle out of his hands. He will most probably try to save himself with one hand, or with both hands, and the Disarm should not be difficult. But if he refuses to let the rifle go you must resort to kicking, jabbing with your knee or heel, punching, etc., until you are able to secure the rifle and make the kill. In any case, do not allow him any respite, and do not let him grab you with his hands, or kick or trip you with his feet.

Should he drag you down with him, keep your body upright and land with your knee well in his stomach. You may "wind" him, but in any case you will be able to force the weapon out of his hands.

The Kill

Having disarmed your opponent, shorten arms. As your hands were in the reversed positions on the rifle when making the Right-Hand Counter-attack, this Shorten Arms position will also be reversed, that is to say left-handed. Without pausing, deliver the death stroke.

Withdraw as after a Trip (and revert to a right-handed guard, if necessary).

Inward Left-Hand Parry

If, armed, you attack an unarmed man and, as you thrust, he parries by pushing your bayonet to his right with his left hand, give him a Right Butt. By pushing your bayonet to your left he begins this stroke for you ; his right hand is well out of the way and he will not be able to make use of it.

55

Inward Right-Hand Parry

If your adversary makes an Inward Parry in the opposite direction, that is to say by pushing your bayonet to his left with his right hand, shorten arms.   By doing this you not only take your weapon out of his reach (and cut his hand if he grasps the bayonet), but you regain a perfect position for thrusting while he is placed in an even worse position than before for stopping you.

Appendix A

Rules and Conventions of Bayonet Fencing

The Fencing weapon has been described in Chapter I. The sticks for Butt Fencing should have their ends padded as described for the " point " end of the Training Stick.

The clothing required for Bayonet Fencing was described in Chapter II ; so were the " Target " and " Hits."

Acknowledgment

When a fencer feels that he has been hit, whether on the target or not, he should " acknowledge " the hit by calling out " Hit !" or " Yes !"—if possible pointing to the spot where he thinks the hit arrived. Because he acknowledges, however, it does not necessarily mean that a hit will be scored against him, or even that the play must be stopped.

Assaults

All Fencing should, as far as possible, be carried out under Competition Rules, though, of course, on many occasions it may be necessary to forgo a number of them. Fencers who are in the vicinity of a bout but who are not actually fencing at the moment should always be willing to act as the Jury, not only with the object of regulating the play in progress, but also to train themselves in what is perhaps the most difficult task of all—Judging.

General Rules

1. Every bout must preserve the character of a courteous and frank encounter.

2. Rough or dangerous play must not be resorted to, and hits must not be aimed at a non-valid part of the opponent.

3. The hand may be used for parrying or for holding the opponent's rifle, but neither the point nor the edge of the bayonet may be touched.

4. Except in Butt Fencing, tripping is not generally permitted, but if a fencer falls to the ground and becomes defenceless a hit will be scored against him.

5. If Simultaneous Attacks are made, resulting in Simultaneous Hits, no hit is scored against either fencer, even if one of the hits was off the target.

6. If for any other reason both points touch at the same moment, a Double Hit occurs and one of the fencers has erred.

Conventions in respect of Double Hits

1. The fencer who is attacked is alone counted as hit if—
    (a) He makes a Stop Thrust on a Simple Attack ;
    (b) He attempts to avoid a hit instead of parrying it, but fails to do so ;
    (c) His return does not follow immediately after his parry ;
    (d) He makes an attack on his opponent's preparation.

2. The fencer who attacks is alone counted as hit if—
    (a) His opponent is holding his point in line and he does not divert it either before or during his attack ;
    (b) He continues his attack after having made a beat which does not find his opponent's weapon ;
    (c) He continues his attack after having been parried ;
    (d) He pauses in the middle of his attack.

NOTE.—If it cannot be decided which of the fencers is the defaulter, no hit will be allowed and the bout will be resumed.

Competitions

Competitions may be held for individuals or for teams. If time permits they should be run on the " Pool " system, but where this is inconvenient the " Knock-out " system can be employed. When the number of entrants is very large, or in the case of large teams, a combination of the two may be expedient.

If weather permits, they should be held out of doors ; in any case, the fencing ground should be an arena 40 ft. square, the outline being marked distinctly by white lines, boards, benches or other means. Starting lines on which the fencers must come on guard are required in the arena, 20 ft. from each of two opposite corners.

The Jury

The Jury consists of a President and four Judges ; it is also permissible to have a Vice-President, but this is not essential.

The President should place himself about twelve feet from the fencers when they take up their positions on the starting lines, and in line with the centre of the arena. It is his special duty to follow the play as a whole and to be able to recall the events of each phase in their true sequence.

A Judge is placed on each side of the President in line with the starting lines ; the other two Judges are placed in similar positions on the other side of the competitors. They must move round with the play, but each Judge should watch the competitor farthest away from him. It is their duty to watch for hits and to indicate, by a movement of the hand, when they see what they believe to be a hit, whether it is on the target or not. The President alone will order the bout to commence or to stop, except in the case where it is necessary to stop it in order to avoid an accident. Play must be stopped for ever hit, unless it is quite obvious that it is not good.

Duration of Bouts

Every bout will last until three hits have been scored agains one of the fencers.

Commencement of Play

Lots having been drawn for ends, the President places the competitors on their respective starting lines. He then orders " On Guard." He asks, " Are you ready ?" and when he receives the affirmative answer from both he orders " Play !"

The competitors are now at liberty to attack ; they may fence in any manner, provided they obey the Rules and Conventions of Bayonet Fencing.

Cessation of Play

Play must cease immediately the President gives the order " Halt !" or " Stop !" No new action may be initiated after this order, but any movement which has already begun may be completed. In the same way that every fencing action which takes place before the order to play has been given is invalid, so every action after the order to stop has been pronounced is null and void. But if a fencer stops before the order to stop has been given and is then hit, the hit is valid unless he stops in good faith and a sufficient interval of time has elapsed without action.

Method of Judging

Having stopped the play, the President asks all four Judges whether the competitor they are watching has been hit on the target, and if the hit was a good one or not. The Judges must answer " Yes " or " No " to the first part of the question, but may qualify this by such expressions as " Too low," " Flat," " Graze," " Hand," etc. If they are not certain they may abstain from voting. If he thinks it necessary, the President may ask for more precise details as to the validity of the hit or as to when the hit occurred ; nevertheless he should delay the play as little as possible for the sake of the fencers. In any case, if the two Judges who are watching one competitor agree, he must accept their judgment.

If one of the Judges abstains, but the other has a definite opinion, the President's own opinion decides the point ; if, however, he has no definite opinion, the opinion of the one Judge who has voted must be taken.

If both Judges have positive but contrary opinions, or if both abstain from voting, the President decides in accordance with his own opinion. If he has no positive opinion, he declares the hit " doubtful." A doubtful hit does not score against the fencer receiving it, but it is sufficient to annul any subsequent action other than a Remise, Redouble or Counter-return.

Crossing the Arena Boundary

The President should warn a competitor when he is about six feet from the arena boundary. If after this warning the competitor steps over the line with both feet, a hit is scored against him. If he has not been so warned, the play is stopped and the fencers are put on guard six feet inside the boundary.

Ground gained or lost

Ground gained or lost is held until a hit is scored, when the competitors are replaced on guard on the starting lines.

Recording of Hits

The recording of hits is normally done by a Scorer who is placed outside the arena. Hits are registered against the fencer hit, not for the one hitting. After a stoppage of play, and before the resumption, the Scorer will call out the score. When there is no Scorer the score will be kept and announced by the President.

Appendix B

Pool System

Except in the case of competitions between teams of more than five fencers each, competitions should be organized on the Pool system, in which every fencer fights every other fencer in the same Pool or, in the case of team competitions, every fencer in the opposing team. (See "Order of Assaults," page 63.)

Individual Competitions

Pools should never consist of less than five or more than ten competitors. If there are more than ten, they must be divided into two or more Pools, the leading competitors of these Pools qualifying for a second round of Pools, and so on to the Final round. The same proportion of competitors from each Pool of any one round must be taken into the following round.

Classification

A victory scores 2 points, a defeat 0 points. The classification in each Pool is decided by the total number of points scored in that Pool. Even if the necessary classification can be obtained before the completion of the Pool, all assaults must be fought off.

If two or more competitors in a Pool score the same number of points, the classification is decided by the number of hits received by them. If equality still exists, the number of hits given decides the classification. In the exceptional case where points, hits received and hits given are all equal, a tie is declared.

Ties

Ties are decided by further bouts between the competitors concerned. For a complete explanation of the method of deciding ties, see the Amateur Fencing Association's "Rules for Competitions."

Team Matches

Each fencer of one team meets each fencer of the other team, but no fencer meets another of his own team.

Each individual victory scores 2 points, and each individual defeat 0 points, the winning team being that which has the greater total of points. In the case where there is equality of points, the total number of hits received by each team as a whole decides the match ; if this fails to give a result the match is declared drawn, each team scoring 1 point.

Team Competitions

The winning team is the one scoring the greatest total of points, and so on for the subsequent places. If there should be equality of the number of points scored by two or more teams in the same Pool, the classification will be obtained from the total number of individual points scored by the members of the teams. If there is still equality, the number of hits received by each member of each team concerned will be ascertained and the team which, as a whole, has received the least number of hits will be declared the winner. Should there still be equality, the total number of hits given by each team concerned, as a whole, will decide.

Knock-out System

This system is for use when teams consist of more than five members each.

Each member of each team will wear an arm-band showing his number in the team, and he will fight only the corresponding number in the opposing team. The captain of a team wears an arm-band marked " C."

Bouts are fought in numerical sequence according to the numbered arm-bands, commencing at 1. The winner of a bout removes his arm-band and gives it to the Scorer immediately the result of the bout is declared, so that, after the final bout, the score can readily be ascertained by counting the fencers of each team without arm-bands.

In a case where no arm-bands have been provided, the Scorer keeps a record of the bouts in the manner shown on p. 67.

Captains of Teams

The captain of a team may or may not be one of the fencers under the Pool system ; in the Knock-out system he will fight his opposite number after the rest of the team have fought if it is necessary to decide the match ; he will not otherwise fight.

Between matches he may change the order in which he wishes the members to fight, and he may alter the composition of his team by drawing upon those nominated as reserves.

During a bout, advice may be given by the captain to any member of his team, but only during intervals between hits.

A caution to one member of a team applies equally to all the members of that team.

The captain of a team is responsible for the behaviour of the members of his team; it is also his responsibility to look after their interests. He must act as liaison between them and the other team as well as the Jury; he must be capable of advising them when required to do so or when he considers it expedient. He must be fully cognizant of the Rules and Conventions of Fencing and the Regulations governing Competitions.

Order of Assaults

The following tables give the order in which assaults should be fought under the Pool system. For Individual Competitions the full table is required; for Team Competitions only those assaults which are printed in heavy figures.

Columns are to be read downward, the second column following on the first, and so on.

5 Competitors (10 Assaults)	
1-4	2-4
2-3	1-5
4-5	3-4
1-2	2-5
3-5	1-3

6 Competitors (15 Assaults) Teams of 3 (9 Assaults)		
1-4	3-4	4-6
2-5	1-6	1-3
3-6	2-4	5-6
1-5	3-5	2-3
2-6	1-2	4-5

7 Competitors (21 Assaults)		
1-4	1-5	3-5
2-5	3-4	1-6
3-6	2-6	2-4
1-7	5-7	3-7
4-5	1-3	5-6
2-3	4-6	1-2
6-7	2-7	4-7

8 Competitors (28 Assaults) Teams of 4 (16 Assaults)			
1-5	4-5	3-6	2-4
2-6	1-7	4-7	5-7
3-7	2-8	1-2	6-8
4-8	3-5	3-4	1-4
1-6	4-6	5-6	2-3
2-7	1-8	7-8	5-8
3-8	2-5	1-3	6-7

9 Competitors (36 Assaults) 3 Teams of 3 (27 Assaults)			
1-4	2-4	3-8	4-5
2-7	1-8	4-7	8-9
5-8	5-7	2-6	2-3
3-6	6-9	1-9	4-6
4-9	3-4	3-5	7-8
1-5	2-5	4-8	1-2
2-8	6-8	2-9	5-6
6-7	1-7	3-7	7-9
3-9	5-9	1-6	1-3

10 Competitors (45 Assaults) Teams of 5 (25 Assaults)				
1- 6	5- 6	4- 7	3- 4	6- 9
2- 7	1- 8	5- 8	8- 9	7-10
3- 8	2- 9	1-10	6-10	2- 5
4- 9	3-10	2- 6	1- 5	1- 3
5-10	4- 6	3- 7	2- 4	6- 8
1- 7	5- 7	4- 8	7- 9	9-10
2- 8	1- 9	5- 9	8-10	4- 5
3- 0	2-19	1- 2	3- 5	7- 8
4-10	3- 6	6- 7	1- 4	2- 3

Preparing the Pool Scoring Sheet

As these sheets are designed for various types of contests (Foil, Epée, Sabre, Bayonet, etc.), it will be necessary to write " Bayonet " in the Combat space at the top ; write also, in the same space, the name of the competition or match. In the Pool space write the number of the round (if any) and the number of the pool.

POOL SCORING SHEET.

COMBAT...Pool

W—Win (2 Points).   D—Draw (1 Point)   L—Loss (0 Points)

NAMES	NOS	1	2	3	4	5	6	7	8	9	10	POINTS	PLACING
	1	X											
	2		X										
	3			X									
	4				X								
	5					X							
	6						X						
	7							X					
	8								X				
	9									X			
	10										X		

PRESIDENT OF JURY...

DATE...

65

The name of each competitor must be written twice on the sheet, once in the left-hand column and once at the top of the column of the same number.

If scoring for a team competition or a match, first write the names of the members of one team, commencing at 1, and follow this by the names of the members of the other team. Bracket the names of the members of each team together and write alongside them, vertically, the name of the team.

Scoring

Let us suppose that No. 3 is fighting No. 8. No. 3 receives a hit. The Scorer makes a mark in the small space at the top of the square formed where line 3 crosses column 8. No. 8 next receives a hit. The Scorer makes a mark in the corresponding space in the square formed where line 8 crosses column 3. No. 3 then receives two more hits, for which the Scorer makes two more marks in the first of these spaces (*i.e.*, where line 3 crosses column 8) and announces No. 8 as the winner, the score being 1-3. He then writes " L " in the line 3 column 8 square, and " W " in the line 8 column 3 square.

It will be noted that in a team competition, as no fencer fights another of his own team, the squares at the top on the left and those at the bottom on the right will be left blank.

At the end of the competition the number of points scored by each fencer will be noted on his line in the " Points " column. The number of points scored is obtained by adding up the number of " W's " in the line and multiplying by two. (One point, for a draw, can only be scored in Bayonet Fencing when there is a time limit.)

In the event of two fencers having the same number of points, the number of marks scored against them can be noted in the " Points " column as well, and if necessary the number of marks scored by them, this being obtained by adding up the number of marks in their respective columns.

Finally, the Scorer completes the " placing " column, the fencer with the greatest number of points being placed first, and so on.

The sheet is then dated and passed to the President (sometimes called the Referee), who checks it, signs it, and announces the result.

SCORING SHEET FOR BAYONET TEAMS
Knock-out System

CONTEST........................... ....Round

....			....		
1					1
2					2
3					3
4					4
5					5
6					6
7					7
8					8
9					9
10					10
11					11
12					12
13					13
14					14
15					15
16					16
17					17
18					18
TOTAL POINTS			TOTAL POINTS		
C					C

WINNING TEAM...

DATE................................ REFEREE...........................

Preparing the Scoring Sheet

The name of the contest and the number of the round are first filled in, and then the names of the two teams are written in the spaces at the heads of the columns, one on the left and one on the right. The first and sixth columns give the numbers of the members of the teams ; the second and fifth are for marking the hits received ; the third and fourth for writing in the points scored.

Scoring

As the members of the two teams fight according to their numbers, each line of the scoring sheet relates to one bout. A hit against a member of the left-hand team is shown by a mark in column 2 ; a hit against his opponent by a mark in column 5. In columns 3 and 4, on the winner's side a 2 is scored and on the loser's side a 0. When there is a time limit and the bout is drawn, 1 point is registered in both columns 3 and 4. (The bout is drawn whenever it is left unfinished, regardless of any hits received by either fencer.)

When all members of the teams, with the exception of the captains, have fought, the points gained by each team are added up and the result entered against " Total Points." Should the number be the same for both teams it will be necessary for the captains to fight. There will be no time limit for this bout, which must be for the same number of hits as were the other bouts.

When the match has been decided, the Scorer will fill in the name of the winning team and the date ; the President of the Jury will check the sheet, sign it and announce the winner.